Small Machine

C❣

Poems by Demi Anter

Write Bloody UK

www.writebloodyuk.co.uk

First edition.
ISBN: 978-1-8380332-3-1

Cover Design by Emma Hursey
Interior Layout by Winona León
Edited by Fern Beattie
Proofread by Fern Beattie
Author Photo by Victor Puigcerver
Interior Photographs by Demi Anter

Quotation on p. 14 from *Berlin: Imagine a City* by Rory MacLean (Weidenfeld & Nicolson, 2014). Used with permission.

German Translation of "Welcome to Berlin!" by Luke Swenson.

Type set in Bergamo.

Write Bloody UK
London, UK

Support Independent Presses
writebloodyuk.co.uk

for you,

keep going
keep going
keep going

Small Machine

Small Machine

I

Arrival

II

Year of Wandering

III

The Long Goodbye

Arriv

I

In this city my own actions became memories, and a part of Berlin's history too, not so much because I did anything of importance here, but because others did, and their deeds became enmeshed in my life.

Rory MacLean

You are crazy, my child. You must go to Berlin.

Franz von Suppé
nineteenth-century Austrian composer

Fifteen Minutes

the plum-coloured stripe around your right knee
marked your first blue kitchen
    the panel that fell & sliced you open
the day you & your best friend deep-cleaned the apartment
(in anticipation of one finally getting laid)

it was after your boyfriend flew home
goodbye kiss lasting until Tegel's gates closed
you, wet-faced, watched him manoeuvre
    the cat through security

it was August
    air heavy
phone buzzing
you screamed
    into the couch
fifteen minutes to find an
    English-speaking hotline
fifteen minutes to tell
    the gentle voice on the other side
        you will not kill yourself

it was one scar of many
    one day
in a too-long-too-short existence
    seconds strung together
pocks & scratches & burns
    sharp kisses pulling skins open
a bodily cartography of
    waltzes
    bike rides
    tumbles onto cobblestone

        Berlin's lonely walks home

Berlin's dawn of swirled raspberry
    that appears sometimes to be
      only for you

    your map

      this body

    tells you to

curse the pain
wipe the blood
    & keep going

Pink Coat

In 1996, I yearned for the ribbon-dancing set
advertised on television between Saturday cartoons.
Imagined our life together: me a ribbon dancer,
satin-swathed in pinks, lilacs, blues,
those streams of colour an extension of
frenetic limbs, girlish energy, my endless potential—

My parents said no.

Now I stare at the pink coat in the shopwindow
like I do every night walking through Mitte.
Dream of soft wool, thick sash tying the middle,
that bawdy colour suited only to some occasions—
unlike the grey puffer I've worn for years,
my navy scarf, my black trainers.

My parents said, *We know you.*
By the time you get it, you won't want it.

In 1996, ribbon-dancing, otherwise known as
rhythmic gymnastics, became an Olympic sport.

I'm still not sure when my want is enough,
how to know I won't get bored.

Open House: Two Rooms

Our rooms feel vast, too-quiet.
The cat's eyes reflecting streetlight
give little comfort, while the great
glass windows cannot help but let in
cold. Every creaking footfall,
every snow-scuffed boot rattles us
that winter.

         And once you return,
      will I be able to stand it, either?

history of love

there's a picture of you— a series of pictures of you— in your mom's office— now your office— where you are young, tow-headed, black and white, inspecting roly-poly bugs.

you pick them up one at a time, admiring and petting and finally releasing each bug back.

there you are, crouched and smiling over the black and white sidewalk, the black and white grass.

Ex at the Museum

I don't pay much attention to the art
   though I like the foggy Richter paintings

and Vija Celmins' comb—
   I think she should have kept making combs—

and the spiders and the Calder mobiles
   obvious as they may be.

I cannot overcome the distance between us there
   moving through the airy tomb.

Something bobs around our heads:

   a history of loving you and being loved by you.

A tour group enters. My favourite Calder sways

   swirling shadows on your patient face.

Yell Out

A field trip to the local college brings
every high school student in the desert
to the same coordinates, on the same
blistering end-of-summer day where I,

sixteen, still unsure if he loves me, walk
narrow alleys formed by school buses,
blonde hair and white skirt pinned between
black asphalt, cloudless sky—

and he, sure of something, pops
his shaggy head out the bus window to
yell out my name. In the beginning,
I feel like an apple, plucked by the sun.

Towards the end, he says we should meet
every ten years— but I'm not sure
when to start counting.
We meet again and again:

Sometimes he has new eyes,
a new voice, flawless new skin,
but when he speaks I hear the same confusion.
His thinks that love is a vanishing.

I think love is a many-headed beast
waiting to fool you into trying.
Lurking under the newspaper, in broom cupboards.
Waiting on park benches, cigarettes drooping
from his glossy mouth.

He's looking through glass for you,
brushing his hair back for you,
an eye on the street and clock ticking down
for precisely the moment to—

Summer Ad Infinitum

I like that you think about
what shoes I should wear,
not heels but white sneakers.

And I like your shoes
even when they're dirty
or strapped to a backpack
on my dining room table.

I have angst about germs
but yours are alright.

Put your head on my shoulder
        kind of germs.
Don't mind the sweat on your brow
        kind of germs.
Hot and crowded on the U8
    and hold my knee anyway
        kind of germs.

You're a germ
and I can already imagine
vacations with you,
gardening on Saturdays,
oozing around the yard
in a smart cap and the kind of shorts
our dads wore in the '70s,

a time when nothing was
more beautiful than
tall / blonde / tan
and the colour red
in an analog print.

So Warm I Cannot Bear to
Move You Away

How can a handful of scenes across two months, one summer,
seem like an etching, stone?

Your side and mine make the bed, dirty towels
strung above French doors, and your eyes shut,
moon-child, dead to the sun until three p.m. or four.
Sleep while I read your books and tan my legs
on the balcony, suspended among trees,
peeling paint, glass bottles and ash.
I count pages like petals— *he loves me*
— he loves me— he just hasn't realised it yet.

Count off days until fall— pages, petals, leaves falling,
    chest falling, crestfallen.
Count domestic scenes in memory: *didn't that happen, didn't it count*
    for something?
Count Augustiners, bruised toes, secrets, perfume samples.

My naiveté sprawls bright and green
and though I know the truth, know the season is ending,
I stay a little longer in your rusting chair,
thumb the pages, waiting for you to see I'm not there
in bed, to raise your shorn head, squint against
sunlight, beam across the room.

You take me in for this long moment then.
I long to know but never learn
what it is you think of me— blurred by sun,
reading books on your balcony—
before you close your eyes
and fall heavy
into moons.

Durch

Tut es weh?

Does it hurt?
he asks, as he presses his finger
into my stomach:
This is where the hate is,
we are going to *release* it.

By my Tante's recommendation
I find myself here, lying on his table,
sweating in September—
Autumn is fickle in Austria.

What strikes me most is
this Austrian guru
seems to know me right away:

He knows I'm an artist.
He knows I'm afraid.
He knows loneliness.
He knows anger is lodged in the stomach.
He knows I spent my summer
    sinking like a stone,
an unrivaled heaviness pressed against my throat
    as I fell deeper and deeper under water,
        the kind of darkness
        your eyes no longer adjust to.

He knows my
    soul
doesn't want to be here,
not Berlin,
not Salzburg,
not anywhere—

Schau mir in die Augen.
Schau dem Teufel in die Augen.

Look me in the eyes.
Look the devil in the eyes.

He smiles and says,
The problem with reincarnation is,
once you escape this life,
the soul just has to keep coming back
    and back and back…

Look me in the eyes a minute longer—

Es ist schön, dass du etwas Gutes in die Welt bringen willst.

Apparently
   my soul
is old and knows,
This too shall pass—
is nothing new,
and this man,
this witch,
this therapist,
this blue-eyed devil
looks in me and sees
I spent my summer searching
for reasons to not kill myself,

that the search was long.

That I still often wonder
if there's a point to it all,
the burdens to carry seemingly unending—

But, now I think the points come
burning through darkness,
bright sparks when we least expect them.

Tut es weh?

It hurt that day
but there were words exchanged
I know to be true:

To make this life worth living,
you must speak loudly,
have courage,
keep going— *durchgehen*.

You must go *through*.

_____

Es ist schön, dass du etwas Gutes in die
Welt bringen willst:
It is beautiful that you want to bring
something good into this world.

Through

I think about calling the hotline a second time my roommate Juan comes home and cries in the bathroom we keep our doors closed today the rooms dark I want to write Vicente just to know that one person thinks of me this second to know I exist

I exist I was getting better but something is going backwards the more I strip away the more I don't like the woman underneath she is not self-reliant or particularly kind

when friends need me I find excuses I fall easily into boredom and self-pity despite the millions of people animals oceans having it worse I am not a hard worker like I thought

maybe I was but the city has changed me with its clanging bells comfortable rhythms its relaxed pace temperate autumns and Sundays

today is a Sunday and there is no place in the world I would like to be but an Austrian spirit guide told me that the only path is forward the only choice to go through

Juan appears in my doorway holding a pile of clothing my clothes are wet I press them to my chest to clear the machine we'll work like this for the evening in the kitchen in silence he'll wash the dirty while I hang the clean.

Smoky Like the Boys

winter is back and with it
the cigarette bitterness
the hazy *Kneipen*

when I come home late, untwist
the scarf from my hair
I smell a Slovenian actor
asking as I leave the party
But we'll see you tomorrow?

I thought twenty-six too old
to be an ingénue but he's even older
— looks like Baryshnikov

There's a new trick to remain an intrigue:
breeze out the door on a wisp of smoke

I shed my coat, remember
the painted wood chieftain
when children were allowed
in tobacco shops and a girl
might help her dad pick cigars
from the case

stretch the jumper overhead—
a picture of you, brooding with cigarette
always brooding always mad

the blouse catches my ears I hear
the question asked one thousand times—
I'm having a cigarette, want to come outside?
and my answer always— yes

yes— though I don't smoke
yes— though I despise it actually
yes— I come home smelling like you but alone
yes— I tossed dad's last pack just to see what floats
yes— I woke with a start, sensing
    something is burning!
    something is wrong!

yes— there is only me in the lamplight

    nothing more than
    the smell of smoke

Kneipen: traditional German pubs

Twenty-Six

And now I am
eating a hard boiled egg with a spoon

And now I am
asking for money again

listening to friends' weekend conquests

And now I am
back in Berlin

calling my mom at all hours of the night

weighing fifty-six kilos with clothes on

trying to answer the hotline volunteer,
their soft, ambiguous voice asking:
*how likely are you to hurt yourself,
on a scale of one to ten?*

And now I am
packing the flat where we lived together,
the *Neubau* with no right angles

locking the door

twisting my body into the ceiling,
brighter than fire,
than disco ball

And now I am
stretching my feet over my head as the teacher says:
slowly, slowly, yoga is breathing

strumming hard, happy when blisters form

tasting the snow

And now I am
on the third floor, no elevator, living with Juan

now: on the fourth floor, living alone

smelling the rain

hiding in the stairwell with Sufjan
five in the morning, crying to high notes

And now I am
not crying as often as I was,

I promise

January 1st, finding all the shops are closed

I give up on buying stamps   float ghostly in the dusk   between
the other New Year's people   dog walking   *Kaffee-und-Kuchen*
breath-mist shudders   little songs for the cold

Try not to think of how happy you seemed   in autumn   how
I heard your laughter long after passing   the crowd on the street
your head thrown back a kind of sun   gleaming

The sky's purples and blues tick us towards four o'clock's
unforgiving dark   I skim my feet against wet pavement until I
hit the stone   dislodged from Earth   waiting   to be set down
between the gaps   to be pressed   gently back

———————————

Kaffee-und-Kuchen: coffee and cake
(a traditional German pastime)

In the Telling of It

My Tinder date says he's a *storyteller*.
He's an actor. I'll never learn.

He hasn't heard of James Joyce but
thinks he's read *Finnegan's Wake*—
Yeah, that one sounds familiar—
once or twice.

Between knee touches and brags
about his time in the military,
he tells me I have *feline features*,
and then, that he's allergic to cats.

He reminds me of a boy I loved
who called me *Honey*,
who felt persecuted by bees.

Months later in a Dublin cafe,
I look up to find Joyce's bespectacled face
baring down from books on all sides,
and I wonder where my love for Joyce began.

I suppose the answer is in pages burning,
pages alight, words a phosphorous strike.
Ash sky. An incandescent army, a river, a flood.
Water in my hands, pulp between fingers.
A language that refuses to stay still.

Joyce didn't care much for convention,
so much so, *Ulysses'* printer stepped in,
refusing to reset type after the third
or fifth rewrite. Unusual language.

Language: easily grown, quickly rotten.
Gift given. My gifts to the honey-boy included:
sad stories, nights sitting on a bench outside
the church and a poem, handwritten,
lined pages torn carefully.

His to me: the reason behind his car accident,
the fallout with his family. *You can't tell anyone.*
So I hold it inside until I feel ugly, swollen like a balloon,
until he is gone and something in me goes, too:
Stillborn, an ending— but not a proper goodbye.

Joyce knew love dies on the page.
That real love is in the telling of it,
the sanctity of tongues,
an intricate dance of risk and mercy,
yours and mine. *I never told anyone.*

Love died, when you stopped saying
what you wanted. And now all's left
is that unsaid. Unfinished words go on
falling gently, gently falling between us.

The untold story stinging endless in my head.

Suspended

I was born on an island
and all my recurring dreams
are of water, the wide
expanse of deadly black,
waves roiling upwards
to overtake the town.

I watch the coast from a hill
in these dreams,
keeping my eyes peeled
for dad and dog,
hoping they'll find the car,
hoping they'll make it out
before the crash—

I wake
waves suspended
over beach and gas station,
over paved road and dirt path,
over room, over my head,

I wake panting like a dog,
like I survived something or
the premonition of something
to come, grumbling, whistling,
unfurling itself before me—
it's bluer than expected,
faster than I could run.

A Cure for the Common Cold

for Patricia D'Alessandro

Honey pours from my eyes
as the mustard dries under
the Band-Aid, poultice yellow—
a flake on skin. I think about
the time I ate a lemon, whole,
rind and pith, spitting the seeds
into a cup because
Patricia told me to.

Patricia the poet, Patricia
the Italian grandmother
with lively dinner parties,
erotic artworks, upright piano.
Patricia never remarried,
never let on in any of her long,
long letters what she regretted.
Patricia died sharp, effusive,
a diamond buried in
Desert Hot Springs.

Meanwhile my mother fights
the first time against
loneliness, that great bear.
We spend Christmas stoking
the furnace, sparks flutter,
burst. Oma swears softly,
Ich hob' kein Mann, while
Opa sits drinking next door.

I'm all for folk cures. *Mutti-Medizin*.
But how, despite centuries
under our belts of stars, ash,
leather, lamplight, silver coin,
silver moon, whale fat, despite
steel rivets and river-red, arcing
across the skyline, despite cells

that multiply under foot and nail-bed,
ecosystems living in my eyelashes,
the keep on keeping on,
    and on and on—

despite that, how have we failed to understand:
Love is a game of fangs, *glänzend und giftig*.

<hr/>

*Ich hob' kein Mann: I have no
husband (Austrian dialect)*

Mutti-Medizin: Mama's medicine

*Glänzend und giftig: glistening and
poisonous*

Women's Work

This poem is for my mother
who (at 157 centimeters) is shorter than me—
but she struts like a rooster,
so seems bigger than anything
the world might throw my way,
awful boyfriends, shady bosses,
the Human papillomavirus—

They all crumble to dust
with a shrug of her tanned shoulders.

She dances tango
studies meditation,
is a little bit good at a lot of things.

She counts them up,

One child, one divorce,
one crazy, Austrian family,
one house of her own
in the Californian desert.

Despite the weather,
she makes things grow.
I like to think about her
in the garden, planting seeds.

I see something of her frame in mine,
feel the ache of the weight she's carried,
duties expected, keeping of secrets,
she carried debts like a wasp in her ear,
the fear of returning to poverty,
a childhood of clothes from garbage bins,
food just expired, *just as good* —

We come into this world alone
but with a rope that ties us to one person—

I see her so clearly:

arms outstretched and a shovel high,
with each strike—
the earth gently snows towards the sky,
with each strike—
expectations eviscerated,
daughter uplifted.

Mother,
my Atlas,

with all of your power
and all of your courage,
how can they dare to call us
the weaker sex?

feel free

stand close to the oven
so your bare legs soak up
the last of the warmth
where you just cooked
the salmon in butter and salt,
three portions to scarf down
between shifts at the vegan donut shop
three afternoons per week
shyly lowering your eyes
when each colleague asks
the inevitable questions:
first time in gastro? American? 27?
what did you do before here? but
are you vegan too? vegetarian at least?
feel the heat on this, your day off
your nothing day, your day of silence,
no one knowing where you are,
no one caring to find out.
glory in warmth blossoming
over pale skin and try—just try—
just try to remember it is okay
to be alone here on this street
whose name you can't pronounce.
to sink your teeth. feel free.

Love Letter to Lou in the Lake

When I drop in this afternoon,
you feed me baked potatoes,
broccoli salad, avocado for butter
because you're trying to be
vegan or something.

You are clever enough to suggest
bringing our bodies to water
on this day we both feel
dull to our bones.

You know the best places to swim,
the ideal gap in the lake's great green
fence to toss our bags and jump in.
Quickly we are sunk in murky blue,
catching light from seven o'clock sun.
It waited for us to set. And I try to think of
a phrase to describe the way your
newly-shaved head bobs along the water
as fat clouds and fatter ducks cruise above.

But no image that comes to mind is flattering.
It sounds rude to say your head is round
like the moon, or slick as a porpoise.
Inflated? Like a ball? Hairless, like a seal?
You'd think I hated you, Lou.

❧

We writers, we try to get to
the truth of the thing.
Truthfully, I still feel empty, often.
Still feel like crushing the inane
people and their inane phrases
designed to give comfort
wherever love has died:

There are silver linings
to every cloud,
to every person.

❧

There are white peaches, I think,
and your head, Lou, is especially this,
gloriously freckled, expertly floating
over golden waves. Plötzensee ripples.
Sunday vignettes around you,
a silver-lining, lake-diving, crash course
in enjoying summer's offerings,
dusk's last words to us both—
as if today were all that mattered,
and it is.

Snowfall in a Pandemic

On the last day of March, the sky mirrors our moods,
a collective *humph*, as we loll and look forward to
weeks, months, years of this shit.

Then, beyond the panes of glass, we see it:

Snow.

The first snow of the year after a fitful, dreamless winter
bursts forth and falls fatter than any we've seen
as we neighbours creep towards windows,
and onto quiet *Balkons*. We reach out to feel ice
melt against skin, grin at each other
across streets and phone screens.

I think of the story from Bulgaria:
Baba Marta shakes out her mattress, spring-cleaning,
the feathers falling are the last snow before spring.
This thick white snow hangs above us, moonsome,
night's shepherdess guides no matter where we look up from.

For one blessed hour, the snow falls over barren branches,
untrod cobblestones. Pillowing paths untouched,
it anoints us as we hold out our hands,
dream for a moment we are together
again.

———————

Balkons: balconies

Porridge

Porridge for the twelfth
damn day in a row; I am
now made of porridge.

Mourning, Day 28

We get through the day as best as we can:
her sleeping in the armchair,
me crying on the couch.

One foot in front of the other—
the only way we know how.

We've done it before,
we'll manage again,

to get through the day
as best as we can.

Not sure if there's a ghost

here, perhaps something
the cat can see flitting on air,
catching light and *Feuchtigkeit*.
High humidity denotes higher presence in the room.

Cats are better attuned to subtle changes,
but maybe we've made adjustments for each other
all along. Hold space for me,
dear ghost.

I would happily host you if only I knew how,
if you could tell me your preference
in the morning: eggs and toast, orange juice,
red wine or black coffee?

My skills are limited but I am trying—
becoming— a version of myself
someone else would want to live with.

Sometimes I stare out the window
waiting for this someone to amble
up my street, marked like some kind of
journeyman for the soul.

Show yourself to me. Don't make me beg.
There's sage in the kitchen drawer
and a friend has offered me
some strong Palo Santo,
but I promise not to use them, yet.

———————

Feuchtigkeit: humidity

To the Dogs

The park down the lane has gone to the dogs. 8 a.m.,
my tender bones twitch towards them,
still chasing rabbits in sleep.

Dogs jostle, a jumble of amour and tail,
shepherds, spaniels, labs, tangled paws of dog joy,
dog laughter, while fifteen *Leute* in black windbreakers—
dog parents on the school run—
clutch coffees and release careful chatter.

I look like one of them but loop the park at a distance,
watch a stout beagle scour the crowd for his old girl,
and wonder what reunites them, what binds them—

a smell, a touch, a click of the tongue?

They know each other, like I hope you know me
when I break from the pack, panting and muddy,
sniffing the air—gasoline—squirrel—*Glühwein*—
oak leaf— cheeks billowing, ruddy,

searching for your smell—
charcoal dust, stockinged-feet,
your hands at the edge of the crowd,
your form knelt down, warm,
waiting to catch me.

Leute: people   *Glühwein: mulled wine*

Tempelhof

I.

What was it like growing up without him?

It's hard to grasp that absence is an abuse,
fear is subtle, coiled deeply inside.

The mind wants evidence.
The mind wants concrete.

I don't have bruises to show you.

II.

I live two-and-a-half kilometers from
the house where my grandfather Rudy was born.

Eight further, my father had his aneurysm
while stationed at the airbase at Tempelhof's *Flughafen*.

III.

Two years ago, I went to Tempelhof to fall in love,
stumbled around Schillerkiez ringing doorbells,
certain he was with someone else
if ever he didn't answer right away.

It was an unbearable summer.

IV.

My grandfather,
the one who grew up to be an engineer,
a sharp dresser— who moved the family to California—
as a child, he took the brunt of his father's dislike,
passed the buck to my father in time.

My father, nineteen
during his unbearable summer.
Nineteen, doing German translations
and writing poems on the side.

V.

I have this breathing problem.

They call it *sighing dyspnea*,
an awareness of the breath
which makes you then unable to—
which sneaks up on you
like a hand on the back of your neck,
so you gasp for air

Es fühlte sich an— als wäre Luft in meinem Hals gefangen—
und ich könnte sie nicht—
ausatmen—

I stammer to doctors in dodgy German.
I'm told to relax but I can't stop thinking about it:

Aneurysm,
inheritance.

VI.

Dear Demi,

I had no prior warning that something was wrong. I had a normal day, and then woke up in the middle of the night — a painful headache, and a brief flashing light with every heartbeat. The entire left field of vision was black except for that small area of flashing. And after that, there was nothing, a blind area, darkness where the light had been. I felt uncomfortable around others and uncoordinated for years. I often could not speak the words I wanted to, as my brain and speech seemed dis-connected. Small stresses would cause me to panic...

In any case, I hope you will never experience a similar event.

VII.

My father was a beautiful man.

It's what the family remembers,
blessed by the occasional visit
when he could get away on leave.

VIII.

I wish I were a beautiful man.

I would have violated others
instead of being violated.

I would have *been* the thing
that I have been searching for,
stumbling around the city
like a dog chases a bicycle.

I would have felt proud
without deserving to be,
and when I wrote poems,
people would have found me
romantic and robust,
instead of feeble or naive.

IX.

Berlin has circled around us,

quietly, waiting,

like that thing in my brain that might burst.

X.

It's strange to me that a city
can hold on to things
like the body does,

this city holds me in
like a breath it won't exhale,

that I, the only child,
would be compelled to return.

When people ask me why,
I can't even remember the reasons—

only that I *always* wanted to,
that it's always been in me.

XI.

The truth:

My father would rather never see me again than come back here.

The truth:

I finally understand why.

XII.

Berlin exists within and without history.

Berlin is a violence. Berlin is a monolith.

XIII.

Move to Berlin.

Throw salt over your shoulder.

Whatever you do:

do not look back do not look over it.

———————————

Flughafen: airport

Es fühlte sich an als wäre Luft in meinem Hals gefangen undich könnte sie nicht ausatmen: It feels like there is air trapped in my throat and I cannot breathe it out

Son of a Fish

The warm morning after I drink four
large Pilsners, I gulp cold water till it spills
over my chin, just resist dipping my head
under the spout, nesting in the blue bowl

of porcelain, while everything around me
is golden— golden, yellow, golden, shining!
Fall has struck me again in the street and I cannot
make a step, nor breathe, for fear of rustling.

We spoke about fathers,
carefully reopening our favourite wounds.
How clever we are to have unravelled their faults,
yet go on doing the same.

I suspect my father spent many days with his head in the sink—

and just like that my taps are open, flowing,
restless, golden. Loner, destined to love him,
or to love like him. Leaf and tree. School of fish.
Swim with the stream. One and the same.

On the weekend Biden wins
the election

I find it hard to feel anything at all.

I shed a wee tear for the celebrations in Ireland,
Ballina and Mary Robinson, leave the house to buy lemons.

Even in Berlin the mood is lighter,
people gather in her parks, buy her bread.

Blonde, brunette, redheaded couples twinkle
in the changing light, maple leaves underfoot

as I finger the yellow net around my lemons
and think about his hands in my hair two nights ago,

how I was left unsure on my long walk home
but now, wonder where he is, what he's thinking

in English or in French. Wonder if his hair
is parted to the right or to the left.

Any poem can be a love poem,
and most poems, indeed, consist of longing,

subsist on lack; no different am I.
Send me a good man so I can show him the door.

Eyelashes

All sanity depends on this: that it should be a delight to feel heat strike
the skin, a delight to stand upright, knowing the bones are moving
easily under the flesh.

Doris Lessing

There was a summer
when my entire field of vision was taken up by
your eyelashes long and fluttering,
your face as you leaned in to kiss me.
I felt myself blossom under your gaze,
I struggled to remember everything that came
before you. This body, all of its years, experiences —
I carry a desert in California, bougainvillea-magenta,
honeysuckle we bit the ends off as kids, rollerblades,
hot cement, knee pads, sunstroke, sweat,
shielded eyes, my mom's visor collection,
hikes up arid mountains, rest houses with facts:
desert tortoise, desert wildflower bloom,
desert oasis we never quite made it to, and mirages—
did they or didn't they exist after all?

I carry reckless jumps off rock piles into spring ponds
and kissing boys in pools, splashing under palm trees,
snorting chlorine, wheezing, laughing.

Enter:
Screaming matches in parking lots, buttons up the back undone,
bows untied, first *love you's*, first drives through Utah,
Colorado, red rock, blue ocean, salt hair, tangled waves
I thought would drown me, losses I thought would drown me,
butter melting, hot bread sizzling, smoking, dancing,
throwing, rowing, shouting, moaning, swimming, floating,

Wandering.

I went wandering and ended up
Here, so I could unfold myself
and all these twenty-eight years,
unzip at the throat and expose to you:
All of it. I wanted you to have all of it.
     I wanted you to touch
Everywhere, all of the places I've been,
all of the sunlight I've seen.
I wanted to sway at the pleasure of light
warming the skin, and you—

I can see you that summer when
my entire field of vision was taken up
by your eyelashes, long and fluttering,
your face as you leaned in
to kiss me.

You felt as good as the sun did
on my skin and I wanted you
to feel it, too.

Clear

I want it to be clear:
I have, like, *a lot* going on at the moment?
I'm actually a pretty successful person?
Have you read my artist C.V.—
it's about 10 pages long now, and I'm only 27?
Can you imagine what I'll have done by the time I'm 35?
Have you thought that far ahead about your life?
No, I didn't think so.

I want it to be clear:
Without you, I'll be fine!
I was grocery shopping the other day and a radical/
bisexual/vegan from Australia hit on me, so…
There's that!

Plus:
Last night I stopped to buy some cannoli—
Well I bought you some cannoli and I bought me some cannoli
but you didn't respond to my texts about hanging out so
I ate all of the cannoli by myself— anyway, listen,
I was buying cannoli and the guy selling me cannoli told me
I was *beautiful* and he asked if we could, like, *hang out* some time?

And I was like:
Thanks but no, I'm kind of seeing someone,
and he was like:
No, no, just as friends!

And I was like: *Hahahahahahahaha!*

"JUST FRIENDS"

I want it to be clear:
You're never going to be *just friends*
with me.

You might be sexy but I am a woman and I have perfect teeth.
I've never had braces, you can ask my dentist, Dr. Waylis—
He's known me since I was a child.

I grew up in California
so I have friends in California,
which means I have *access* to California,
and *everyone* wants to go to California
so maybe I'll take *you* to California
but you'll have to WORK for it—
work really HARD for my ACCESS
to CALIFORNIA— just to be clear.

I love sex and I expect my fair share.
I can cook if you can clean.
I have good genes and might deign to pass them on,
to birth, like, 2.5 beautiful children,
but only if *you* take care of them because
Mama will be busy making it rain,
fulfilling her own potential,
coming home late to a tall glass of Scotch
and a leather armchair because
times have changed and
I am your Mama AND
your Absentee Father Figure now—
just to be clear!

Oh?
What's that?
My job sucks?
I have pennies to my name?
Well that's…

…

True?

But you know what?

I am working on it:

I HAVE DREAMS!!!

I know that my housing situation isn't the most stable,
like at the moment I'm carrying a suitcase
back and forth across Berlin
to avoid staying with my now-ex-boyfriend.

But like…

…at least I have *my own* suitcase.

I want it to be clear:

These little hiccups
on the timeline of 2018
do not *define* me,

just like my parents' divorce
does not define me,
my dad's alcoholism
my mom's depression
my grandma's anxiety

DO NOT DEFINE ME!!!

Nor does the Big Break Up of 2009
(thanks to years of therapy),
nor the death of my idol, David Bowie
(who I never got to see in concert, FML,
I discovered his music the year after his final world tour)—
that doesn't define me either!!!

Listen—

The thing about hardship and tragedy
and pulling yourself up by your bootstraps, kid,
because this is your home now, Oliver,
and you only get *this much porridge* is that:

it all makes you Stronger,
and I'm, like, so fucking strong now,
just to be clear—

I can lift a car to save a baby,
I can punch an assailant on the street,
I can make my voice really *really* LOUD:

I AM SO POWERFUL
I ONCE WAS USING POWER TOOLS
AND SHOT MYSELF IN THE FINGER WITH A NAIL
    GUN
AND THEN I TOOK A PAIR OF PLIERS AND
PULLED THE NAIL OUT FROM MY FINGER
I HAD NO CHOICE
NO ONE WAS THERE
I COULD NOT CRY OR STOP TO THINK ABOUT IT
I COULD NOT DRIVE TO THE HOSPITAL
SO I PULLED OUT THE NAIL
AND IT HURT LIKE HELL
AND I BLED ALL OVER THE STUDIO
THEN I WRAPPED THE WOUND IN PAPER TOWELS
WENT TO A MEETING
DIDN'T TELL ANYONE WHAT HAD HAPPENED —

JUST TO BE CLEAR ABOUT WHO YOU ARE DEALING
    WITH,

I don't need you to like me,

but jesusfuckingchrist,
if you did like me like I like you
I would probably do anything
you asked of me
ever—

Just to be clear.

II

*Year of
dering*

There is notoriously nothing more to be said on the subject. Every one has been there, and every one has brought back a collection of photographs… It is not forbidden, however, to speak of familiar things…

Henry James,
'Venice'

She often revisits images of herself single, in the streets of cities where she has walked… These are her selves, it seems to her, who continue to exist in these places.

Annie Ernaux

For Venice

Sparkling phrases chime against wine glasses as every Italian
student of philosophy buys the next round. She keeps up.
Then they're sitting at his table, the kitchen bathed
yellow-green, jazz playing, a joint orbiting, notes on Nietzsche,
Kant, Foucault swirling up the check-papered walls.
She keeps up. Someone has stolen an orange,
someone is in the toilet discreetly throwing up,
someone's glasses fogged, someone says, *Take
the spare room*. She keeps up until
she gets the spins, in a flurry of zippers and buttons
flashes into the night. A bit lost and not so scared,
she finds dead ends, then black waters
edging her forward. She finds her way slow—
more like submarine than *traghetto*— suede gloves swim
through the famous winter's fog. In the morning
she finds orange peels in her pockets. She kept up
with the city that took care of the girl after all.

_____

Traghetto: water bus

The Ship Room

I trace the streets from uptown
down like lines on my palm. Amsterdam
could fit in a pocket. Canals glint,
I hold myself from falling in
while jumping promises—
If I still feel this bad in a month…

It's the weed talking, maybe,
a coffee shop spliff I nurse all weekend
after the tattoos, before
the Rijksmuseum where the pain
subdues as I wander between
wooden ships— mini, medium
and massive balsam models.

I don't remember the wall text,
just being alone in a midnight
blue ocean, its dozen floating
carcasses.

They are lit carefully like dead things
should be, so I don't think of my own ribs
pulsing, the hull of my human body
very much alive. I only think of you,
how you would have liked the ships,
your volumes of war history
made physical.

I'm startled when I lift my sleeves
that night: plastic wrap, ink seeping,
tiny flecks of blood. The needle's sting
was less than the sinking fear,
my loneliness, passing beautiful houses:
spindly creatures with russet mouths
yawning open, lit like churches,
like live things should be.

Plum

I dream of returning to Lanzarote
walking barefoot over black crust

rising alone in the red yurt's heat
plum at the center of the dumpling

catching blue sun over volcanic dunes
mountain shadows into rippling pools

in nightdress I scuttle to the beach
shake the humming from my head like sand

the drone that says *this will end*
and resist the urge to go with the tide

though it would be tidy
to be born on and die on

an island

a plum in my mother's arms
a child at the breast of the long dark sea.

Sabina

I am following Sabina and her teenage sister through Wrocław
to the drag show where queen Babcia Chlamydia will teeter
from the stage to the alleyway to tower over us, welcoming,
neon signs illuminating her gleaming mouth; I am following

Sabina through the Berlin sex club film shoot where we first met,
tripping over beds before our eyes adjust, avoiding a fingering from
the man in the priest outfit; and then to the last old club in East Berlin
where we walk arm in arm to keep upright;

We are too far from home to fight the ten-euro cover
so I follow Sabina to the floor and we throw ourselves into
DJ Vampyre's obscure '80s set, feeling obnoxiously young and hot,
watched by the room; I follow Sabina to every good indie *Tanzparty*

to touchdown in Berlin between 2016 to 2020: to Privatclub's
red walls and frisky bankers, Internet Explorer's French disco,
Humboldthain's carpet of cigarette burns, 8mm's film projections,
Loophole where we hide from past flings, arkaoda's dazzling basement,

Columbiahalle for posing in faux fur coats—we *Tanz*'ed them all;
I follow Sabina to Zalando where we share a desk and international gossip,
where I quit before my trial period ends, ignoring her advice;
Sabina follows me, trailing as I walk ahead down every Neukölln side street,

Weserstrasse to Wildenbruch— as if I know where I'm going;
Sabina complains, mounts her bike, an act of defiance
(and the only way she'll keep up); then it's May or June, and we round
Tempelhof's reclaimed runway, circling each other

in the steamy evening, peach sky; we piss each other off
when I am Californian (stubborn and idealistic) and she is Polish
(practical and stern), but hash it out on the dance floor,
over Facebook Messenger, on third-floor balconies, rarely

but sometimes crying for uncertainty, for the ticks towards/past Thirty;
asking which jobs, which boyfriends, which cities
will make us happiest; I am following Sabina's deep inhale when
we are stopped by Polish police for drinking on the street

and I've forgotten my passport; the exhale as the last train leaves
without us. I am following Sabina with my lens; I take one of her
and she one of me— on the ferry, red sunglasses, chalk blue sea;
I am following Sabina's gaze over Copenhagen where we climb

Our Saviour's swirly spire, swim the salty river and drink cans
on the way home; when it's dark in the trees and we are alone
she says, *I don't mean to be rude, but I need to tell you*— so I hold breath,
waiting for her hammer to come down—

I need to tell you, Demi, that this is the best trip EVER!

The woods spit us out into the warm, waiting, warbling city,
where we are laughing tears and crying laughter, streetlights
waving gold for its two funny girls, one of us always slightly ahead.

————————————

Babcia Chlamydia: Grandma Chlamydia   *Tanzparty: dance party*
(name of a drag persona)
                                          Tanz'ed: danced

City Girls

We crouch, raincoats crinkle
in the tall grass of the field.
Hands out, open–palmed, silent,
eyes nearly closed, breathless
as they approach. Gosha is the first
and as she saunters between,
we squeeze back excitement
to crumple the greyish wool,
to marvel, how thick and how
damp! Blessed are those
the sheep choose. To be pet.
We hold our tongues, rain and
sweat pooling on foreheads,
baby-hairs matted as we try to be
present, breathe in deeply
peat and gnats. Dreaming
of a world where we must not
go back.

Who Else but Her?

for Müttilein

Her heart an Austrian passport,
    U.S. green card pinned inside,
her ears prefer loving words,
her nose: Europe's sweet coffees,
her tongue: liquor by noon.

    Last June,
her legs went to Mexico
    to sip Margs by the pool,
    Even in sleep,
her feet never stop tangoing.

    Out on the floor
her arms float, sizzle, tangle. Complicated and magical,
    Borges should have written a story about her, all the men
    that fawn, awaiting their turns at the *Milonguera*,
her laugh a horn blast while she careens out the port.

    And though
her advice is sometimes a jar of jam left sitting
    in the armpit of my fridge, that laugh
    splits floorboards, summons the dead.

I hear it curling up to rest in the walls,
I hear her waiting until I need her again.

———————————

*Milonguera: a woman who spends
a lot of time dancing tango at social
events, e.g. "Milonga"; also a type
of tango dance style*

did you hear about mom?

did you hear about the time mom danced all night in prague?
she was in love with a saxophone player and, by proxy,

all saxophone players. jazz made her feel alive and warm even as
the snow fell on cobbled roads and she and paulina left faint trails

with their boots on wet stones. there's a video, you know the one!
mom struts through the empty street, sheds her gloves,

throws her raincoat to the floor. there are more, thirty-five millimeter
scans from the trip to lanzarote where she slept in a blood-red yurt —

feeling the colour would soothe her yearning heart — and hiked across
black rocks while waves crashed, her mustard dress flapping wild,

white adidas ash-caked. the route brought her to a lava cave,
lavish and romantic where she ate alone, and listened to, you guessed it,

saxophone. there are photos from home, velvet coat and orange scarf
draped just so. clearly hungover in last night's patent-leather shoes.

full of style, the year she worked for the fast-fashion conglomerate,
and nearly stayed on just to stock her wardrobe. the year she almost

killed herself, ideating, calculating force — *(f) = m x a, where m is mass
and a, acceleration* — of trams and trains and small, german automobiles.

she was glad she hadn't killed herself, the night she met the guy
who looked like david bowie, with decent coke and a perfect body

and a grin, she swears to god, could make the sahara desert wet.
there aren't pictures of that, but there's a film from mom's first trip to italy.

she's on the back of aunt lisa's vespa, hair flying and helmet shiny-pink.
mom was glad, then, she hadn't jumped in front of the train in milan.

mom was glad a lot, even in her laurie anderson post lou reed melancholy,
her splintered phone screen days, her delayed flights and summer lakeside

break up despair, truth searching, lobster-red sunburn, blame it on the
mushrooms days. mom was glad at schloss schönbrunn, to have no one else

to care for, to stroll the grounds at her leisure, to wear a red beret.
    and in venice,
to celebrate her own birth without witness, to celebrate by crying in
    cathedrals

and smiling at the boats. mom trusted strangers and floated through
house parties and often chose to walk the last blocks home,
    to talk to herself,

to commit to memory. mom did a lot of things you wouldn't believe.
thought a lot of thoughts she wouldn't dare repeat. but she did
    write it all down.

We haven't gone to Rome yet

The windows above Campo de' Fiori are still closed

the pigeons chatter to themselves unperturbed

by our names riding on sweet pockets of air

you haven't yet left the bruise on my top lip.

We haven't inspected Bernini's Daphne

nor walked Villa Borghese

haven't nestled in its tender grass

barefoot and flushed under shadows of cluster pine.

We haven't gone to Rome yet so I cannot ask

whether we looked more like lovers

or small children

waiting for the afternoon to pass.

The
Good

III

We're lovers, and that is a fact.
Yes, we're lovers, and that is that.

David Bowie

Berlin, you are my body, tired
but unfailing, unflinchingly
resilient. You are, perhaps,
my soul—

Gianluca Avanzato

Sehr geehrte Damen und Herren,

Welcome to Berlin! It is so nice that you want to make your home here. We are writing to inform you that your application has not been successful. Either you have provided too much information or too little. For the sake of your privacy and ours, we cannot say which of those is the case.

Therefore, please use the attached pin code to re-start your application online, whereupon you will receive a letter to complete the process offline, whereupon you will receive a second pin code whispered into your ear by your local Döner man.

In case you encounter problems along the way, please call our hotline, which is open for your convenience between 9 a.m. to 9:30 a.m. every other Wednesday, excluding Asparagus Season.

If you email us, expect to receive a response in 5 to 25 business days via post. This will confirm that we have received your query, but will not answer your questions. For that, maybe try calling again.

If you should get through to one of our representatives, please have all previous communications with our office on hand as we cannot be expected to keep track. Please note that your representative may give advice that conflicts directly with past advice, and/or with advice you may receive in the future. Stay on your toes!

If you have decided you would rather kill yourself than live in Berlin any longer, you may now download the correct form online at: https://service.berlin.de/dienstleistung/210116/selbstmord. Please keep your reasoning under 250 words.

If you fear consequences, you might avoid checking your postbox but we can assure you, this will result in further consequences. We recommend hastily opening letters in the stairwell– if not snatching them directly from your post-deliverer's hand.

Please note that this letter is valid no matter your personal level of German comprehension. Foreigners may well contribute hours of labor and substantial tax revenue, keeping our lights on and elevating Berlin to a world metropolis that attracts the petty bourgeoisie like moths. But we are still in Germany, dig it?

When it comes time to pay up, the only language we are interested in is cold, hard cash. Find the ATM in the lobby. No change given. Don't even ask about the fee.

Thank you for helping us maintain a sense of order, and for your understanding that sometimes to go forwards, you must go backwards. So far backwards that our heads have become stuck. Send help. We are becoming faint from the fumes.

Mit freundlichen Grüßen,

Ihre Stadt Berlin

Sehr geehrte Damen und Herren,

Willkommen in Berlin! Es ist eine wahre Freude, dass Sie hier eine Heimat finden wollen. Allerdings müssen wir Sie informieren, dass Ihr Antrag abgelehnt worden ist. Entweder gaben Sie uns zu wenige Informationen oder zu viele, Genaueres können wir Ihnen nicht verraten. Wir nehmen Ihren Datenschutz todernst.

Verwenden Sie die hier beigefügte PIN, um Ihr elektronisches Bewerbungsformular zu beginnen. Infolgedessen werden Sie einen Brief zum elektronischen Online-Bewerbungsverfahren offline vervollständigen, infolgedessen Sie eine zweite vierziffrige PIN erhalten, um Ihr Online-Konto zu öffnen, diesmal erhalten Sie es geflüstert von einem schüchternen Dönermann mit Hobel.

Falls Sie Schwierigkeiten haben, rufen Sie bitte unseren Hotline-Service an, wir stehen Ihnen gerne zur Verfügung, von 9 bis 9:30 Uhr jeden zweiten Mittwoch— Servicedienst während der Spargelsaison ist nicht garantiert.

Haben Sie bitte Geduld, fünf bis fünfundzwanzig Werktage sind für eine Rückmeldung auf Ihre E-Mail per Post zu erwarten. Dieser Brief wird ausschließlich zur Bestätigung des Erhalts Ihrer Nachfrage dienen— keine Antwort auf Ihre Fragen darf hier verraten werden. Versuchen Sie es gegebenenfalls telefonisch.

Falls Sie in Kontakt mit unserem Service-Personal kommen, werden Sie alle vorherigen betreffenden Kommuniqués vorhanden haben müssen. Wir können diese nicht zur Verfügung stellen. Verstehen Sie, dass es sein kann, dass unser Service-Personal Rat geben könnte, der mit früheren Ratschlägen direkt im Konflikt steht, und/oder damit, was Sie in der Zukunft hören könnten. Bleiben Sie wachsam!

Falls Sie sich entscheiden, dass es besser wäre zu sterben als noch einen Tag in Berlin zu bleiben, können Sie das entsprechende elektronisches Formular herunterladen: https://service.berlin. de/dienstleistung/210116/selbstmord. Bitte begrenzen Sie Erklärungsgründe auf 250 Wörter.

.

Wenn potenzielle Folgen Ihnen Angst bereiten, können Sie einfach Ihren Briefkasten vermeiden. Wir garantieren Ihnen, dass dies weitere Folgen bringt. Wir empfehlen Ihnen, dass Sie Briefe leise öffnen— oder Sie nehmen sie direkt aus des Boten Hand.

Seien Sie aufmerksam: Dieser Brief ist gültig, ob Sie ihn lesen können oder nicht. Trotz der Arbeit und wesentlicher Steuern, die von Ausländer*innen abgenommen werden, was dann wiederum dieses Büro beleuchtet, was dann wiederum Berlin zur Welt-Metropole erhebt, zum Licht, das Kleinbürgertum wie Motten anzieht: vor allem ist der Boden deutsch. Begraben Sie Ihre Hoffnungen hier.

Letztendlich ist die einzige Sprache Kohle. Den Geldautomat finden Sie schon im Wartebereich. Wir haben kein Kleingeld. Fragen Sie lieber nicht nach der Gebühr.

Danke, dass Sie Ihren Beitrag ordentlich leisten und umso mehr dafür, dass Sie Verständnis haben – manchmal muss man für jeden Schritt vorwärts zwei Schritte zurückgehen. Manchmal vier. Manchmal zehn.

Mit freundlichen Grüßen

Ihre Stadt Berlin

limoncello

wait outside Lina's apartment on the wooden bench, reading—
she arrives and loops her arm through mine as if we're sisters or
lovers, as if it hasn't been over a year since we last—

round the corner for Italian, a small table inside— lasagna is fine,
though the conversation unfurls, magnificent— her triumphs, my
woes— bright lights we see in each other, dark nights of the soul—

waiters offer us limoncello— another and another and I am having
a conversation with myself in the bathroom— *DO NOT DRINK
ANY MORE*—

return to find the candle burned low— goblet of wax— Lina
gestures to the newly filled limoncello glass—

sip and laugh about magicians, actors, fires we've tried to tame,
others we've had to coax out— *desire and contentment*, she says—
and, *go to England!*—

at midnight we embrace the waiters short of kissing their cheeks—
turn and wave as we go arm in arm into the night— wanting to
believe we'll see each other again soon—

tram home my phone dead eyes closed dizzy head leaning against
the BVG-yellow railing—

could life be better elsewhere? could not close my eyes on the
Tube, could not slosh upstairs into an apartment of my own— no
Lina to run into at the market— no free limoncello— Berlin's
not far, I know— head absolutely ringing with bells, chorus of
droning— *should I be, should I become*— lie in bed feeling lost
feeling everything at once—

I've learned so much just this year, I say to Lina over lasagna,
swilling sauce— *can there still be so far to go?*

Lina shakes her halo of sunflower curls, her glow casting light about
the room, and says— *it never ends, it never ends, it never, ever ends*—

If God Were German

Yes, well, there's a certain order to things—
you're born, you learn, and, when you're old enough,
you contribute to the State, have a family,
and, one day, if you're very lucky,
you get a pension and a *Schrebergarten*.
If you're very, very lucky, your kids bring you to Mallorca,
and, one day, you die, surrounded by those you cared for,
die in peace knowing you did everything correctly.

You never crossed a red *Ampel*.
Never walked in the bike lane. You were *angemeldet*.
Never sublet without permission or rode the U-Bahn
without a ticket. Your conversations couldn't be heard
by strangers, your music never disturbed the neighbours.
You felt appropriate shame to be German,
learned enough English to travel,
met enough Brits/US-Americans to feel superior.
You never elected a fascist or forgot to separate compost from
        plastic,
clear glass from green, kept the *Restmüll* clean.
Never dared use someone else's bins,
or left shoes in the stairwell.
Never tried to pet other people's dogs.
You got *geimpft* when they called for your age bracket.
(When he took a leftover dose one month ahead of schedule,
you agreed it made sense for Halle's 64-year-old mayor to resign.)
You always paid cash, never cut the line.

And when your heart peters out, your lungs seize,
you think, if God were German dying would be easy:
A stamped *Formular*, a Green Light.

Even so, life doesn't feel too short since
you have always been on time.

Ode to Sommersprossen

Sommersprossen. Lieblich —
German ribbons into eardrums, like a finger
circles around a thumb, like a tongue
licking salt from the glass.

Not a beautiful language! I disagree.
German children sound like school bells
with their fluttering enthusiasm, teak melodies,
crystal high notes.

German is something between metal
and driftwood, strict but irregular, and porous
if you allow your eyes and ears and mouth
to approach. If you don't understand this,
how can we begin to move forward?

And how will I bear to move out,
to let this language, my second brain,
atrophy and die. No *Späti, Schatz* nor
Stein. Barzahlen. Glückwünsche.

There will be nights in England and America,
when I am asked to speak, bring the accent out
to trot along the garden path:
What an unusual language. What an ugly skill.
What a big forehead you have.

How boring, how limited, this English—
not my mother's tongue, nor my father's—
but the one pressed down to them. They
held out open, sweaty hands. *In Berlin geboren.*
There's no good word for *WG, wackelig* or

   schade.

Schaden,

I will miss your shades on my lips
and your crackling in my throat. I will
try to be both, but miss being *beides,*
I will forget how.

I will forget the *Unterricht,* German for losers.
Schade, for fear is not the reason to stay—
it is often the sign to go. So *jetzt: Hüpf, draußen,
mit deinen schönen Sommersprossen!*

Wherever *zuhause,* you will always be my home.

---

*Sommersprossen: freckles (literally,
"summer sprouts")*

Lieblich: lovely, dear

*Späti: liquor store, short for Spätkauf
or "selling late"*

Schatz: sweetie

*Stein: traditional stoneware mug
for beer*

Barzahlen: to pay by cash

Glückwünsche: congratulations

*In Berlin geboren: born in Berlin (like
my Opa Rudy)*

*WG: short for "Wohngemeinschaft;"
an apartment shared by multiple
housemates*

*Wackelig: shaky, wobbly, loose; to
describe an unsteady connection*

*Schade: "That's a shame" or "That's
too bad"*

Schaden: damage

Beides: both

Unterricht: lessons, teaching

*Jetzt: Hüpf, draußen, mit deinen
schönen Sommersprossen!:
"Now: Hop, outside, with your
beautiful freckles!"*

Zuhause: at home

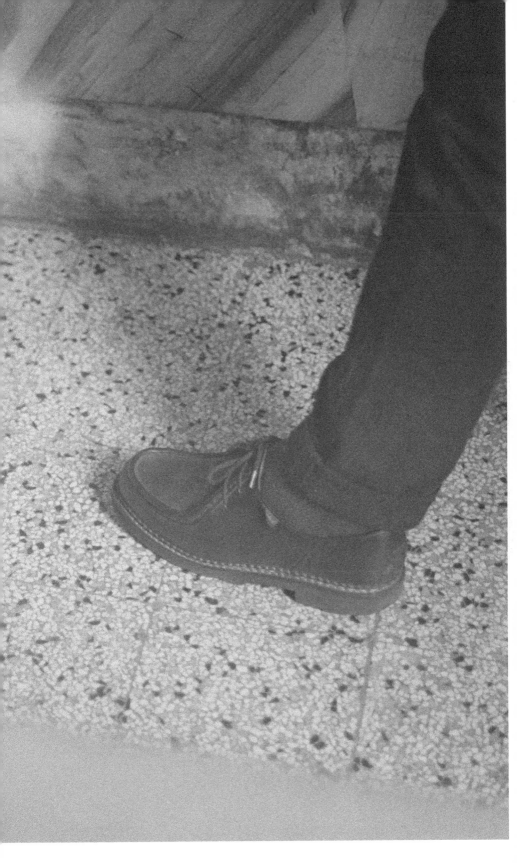

David Bowie Says *Woah*

Today he is nice.
The cup is small but he's
hand-cranked the coffee
and isn't that swell?

I can't be bothered with
Mokka pots but most sexy
men in this city have them,
and he is tall, lean, with
the same smirking mouth
and high cheekbones
as David Bowie. And
David Bowie was sexy.

I savour the weight of
dusky sheets, the mattress
inches above the floor on
palettes, the lushness of
contact, guessing correctly
that this will be the last time.

I will recall whiskey and
piano keys, banging on at
four in the morning— to hell
with his six flatmates, I never
met them anyway— and
honest-to-God candlelight
flickering down the watery
taper, wisdom melting.

We don't love each other,
the truth is we barely speak,
but this morning, from bed,
Bowie and I scream, *Woah!*
as past his window a little
squirrel leaps between oaks,
slides down the branch and

just catches on. We watch,
open-mouthed, this flier
defy death. Humbled and
earth-bound, we are prepared
only to fall into the open earth
of each other. It's late November.
I don't know what he'll remember.

I Know How to Love

I.

I want to bring you something
on this, the final date, to mark
my appreciation, give thanks,
say bye. Perhaps that film magazine
you were interested in or another
book on writing stories.
In the kitchen there are germini
flowers I could un-vase and
carry dripping. There are grapes
in the bowl, but below the bright
bitter skins, the flesh is grey, sloppy.
I thought about Guinness in a can,
but it doesn't taste the same.
I would write you a poem.
It won't taste like me.

II.

After saying goodbye,
I witness a parting embrace
his ear on her cheek,
her free arm dragged down by
a mammoth canvas bag, beckoning
adventures ahead and apart.
I move past while they hold on in their
enchantment. In the end, I brought you
nothing. Now Berlin enters spring:
The wind whirls dust and pollen
through all the Sunday ice-cream-eaters,
their sweaty faces, their children,
the little beige dogs on red leashes.
My face is sweatier than the rest,
blood pools in my sore nose
and I squint upwards, wishful,
as if this could persuade
my tears to cease.

Ty

I never wrote a poem for you,
did I? Somehow we were too
busy talking, no time to write
down the words that tumbled
out whenever we sat across
a table, or embarked on a
drive. Perhaps we were
writing in action, every quiet
movement a couplet to memory.
The poem for take-out sushi
brought to campus around
midnight. The poem for
finishing junior year,
letting me lay in your bed
and play Skyrim for ten
hours/seven days straight.
The one of Berlin and Amsterdam,
barely knowing each other,
and beers along the canal
and fucking in hotel showers.
There are poems for hanging
pictures in our first apartment.
There are poems for birthday
gifts, some failures (paragliding
lessons) and many more successes
(the mandolin, the drill). So
many poems for donuts,
ice creams, loving distractions.
A couple for Thanksgiving,
me never knowing what to
say to your parents. The poem of
your dad's fall. The poem of
your flaking skin, your falling
hair, not knowing how to
take care, not knowing how
to back off. There's a poem

for flying to Germany,
another for our two cats,
all the care poured into them,
all the bowls tipped over.
There's a very long poem
in which I say goodbye.
There's too much to love
about you to write in a poem.
There's too much you
for a text of any length
to capture. Poetry, like
people, has its shortcomings.
But let's not dwell on ours.
We did quite well, you and I.

Holding

To
hold
a dog
is to feel
something solid
like
a little mountain
or a fir tree,
a slice of earth if you will,
that, when pressed,
gives way to softness,
a pressure against the chest,
a warmth and ease.

To hold a cat can be challenging,
the way holding someone else's toddler
can be challenging. Some wriggle,
have a poor attitude,
others scratch. Few are certain and fat. Some
smell delicious like dirt after rain.

When you are ready to carry,
when you are ready to hold,
just know when it's time
to let go.

I Have Become the Kind of Person Who Takes Her Cat to the Acupuncturist

The acupuncturist nimbly slips
a needle into one ear, then the other,
adorning her velvet forehead
as if pinning a jeweled brooch.

All those years ago, I lifted her from her hiding place,
towel fortress where she slept next to brother, sister.
She gave me a look to say, *This is bullshit*—
surprising skepticism in the eyes
of one not yet ten-weeks-old.

She's grown to 89 cm, nose-to-tail,
weighs more than a bowling ball,
moves like a submarine through the *Altbau*
apartment, slow and elegant.

I only hear her when she runs,
pat pat patting over scuffed wood floors
in search of moths and bees.

The cat who's done California, Berlin,
watches me pack boxes for London,
judging my whims with slitted eyes.
When I finish, we sit in the sill,
I watch her watching birds
wilding their wings beyond the glass.

In a basement office, I hold her feet
in solidarity. The acupuncturist guides the qi
around her silky body.

We count to retrieve them all—
two: shoulders, four: hips, six: ankles,
ten— eleven— twelve— thirteen needles.

The doctor tells me about Maine Coons,
their predisposition to hip dysplasia,
their quirky personalities,
while her bearded chin
pokes into my palm,
sharp eyes soften.

I promise,

In London, Gus, there will be a garden,
  tall grass to run through.

Altbau: Literally an "old building."
In Berlin, an Altbau usually refers to a
building or apartment within a building
constructed before 1945, characterised
by high ceilings, ornate stairwells, and
pine floorboards.

In London, Far Away (I Carry You Around for Good Luck)

The grey squirrel with a berry in its paw is good luck,
    the lollipop lady waving me across is good luck,
    missing the too-full train is good luck,
    getting stuck in cold, sticky rain is good luck.

As you know, bad things come in threes— that's my luck,
    but you not writing for three days is good luck—
    I'll convince you that I'm right with good luck.
    Just in case— carry berries in hand.

Fog had entered the home

Rain for ten days and bread
for one. Croissant and *Brötchen*
toast breastbone as I crest the stairs.

I woke, the cat's white
toes nestled in my ribcage.

Through stained glass,
my landlord sweeps leaves
into piles, his hearing aid
glinting.

A honeybee thrums against glass,
small machine, summoning thunder,

And I am in a dream where
Sam's cheek is pressed
against my thigh,

But there in time to open the window,
scold the cat, gather in my arms
the rolling quiet of her fur.

Sometimes I think I dreamt it all,
these years, the rain and the men
and the bread from the corner shop,
the cat who rests her chin on my chest
each morning, waiting for my eyes to
crescent open, the bees released, ungrateful,
never bothering with goodbyes.

Brötchen: bread rolls

Suddenly, Birds

For the first time,
I can tell you the exact date
the buds blossomed.
For the first time,
I was paying attention, aware
of how unaware I had been,
apathetic toward the natural
order of things.

It's been a week and the trees
in the courtyard are already
full of flowers, bustling
yellowish-green.
They reflect light so sharply,
it hurts to look too long.

Eyes burn. Tears come,
sometimes for the brightness,
mostly for the birds. The birds
have suddenly returned home
and flit like stars might
given the chance to wander,
delight from every angle,
constellate.

In this washout spring,
I am grateful for every reminder
that some things never change.
Worlds whir fast and slow and
others go on in their rhythm,

thrilled to be bobbing on a tree,
examining every angle of the branch.

Small Machine

There is a part of me that lifts
when I step onto a tarmac:

The rows of budget aircraft lined up
and gleaming, smile like white teeth in a
handsome head, unperturbed by the grey morning
nor the surly stewards in their clashing uniforms.

I remember there is no better way
to enter a new year than to not know
where you're heading.

The wings lift.

The heart is a small machine
that keeps ticking.

And to think that all along, hidden from our sight, our lives were this small: the world we live in but almost never see; the way we must appear to the hawk and to the gods.

Alain de Botton

Twenty-Nine

And now I am
landing for the last time

from above, roads look like rivers in pitch
drivers swim through forests via red and white light streams
towards families / lovers / children
in the city I called home for five years

And now I am kissing goodbye
the summer we spent swimming
our WhatsApp group pinging sixty times, every hot Sunday
for Teufelssee, Langer and Plötzi

and now I am Cat's sunburned cheeks
as she tells me to go meet another actor

and now I am sore and full of myself:
he played Romeo, baguette emoji, sweat emoji

And now I am eking out spring
on the bench with Sam
shivering
clutching coffees
until we must embrace over
bicycles
bye

And now I am fine on my own
I learn that in the checkout line at Edeka

And now I hardly cry at all

in fact
I am trying to remember how

And now I am
landing
in
snow
the taxi driver swims us into the bloodstream
Berlin's heart flashing red, white

I press my face into the frozen glass
until it fogs
one sentence I can muster:
Schnee gefällt mir

I want to kiss her cheeks
that girl
twenty-four and alone
with just a suitcase of bad German

she should have cried

sighed instead and
strained to see her new city
through the flurries

there it was
rising glittering from the dark

And now we've gone
('til we return)

And now we're fine

Schnee gefällt mir: I like snow

Acknowledgements

I am indebted to countless friends, poets, teachers, and rock idols for their help in making this book real, and, more importantly, for keeping me going during difficult times.

I first of all need to thank the volunteers and organisations that make themselves available to those in need of a listening ear.

If you find yourself in need of someone to speak to, here are the numbers to call:

UK/Ireland: Samaritans 116 123

Germany: Telefonseelsorge 0800 111 0 111

US: National Suicide Prevention Lifeline: 1 800 273 8255

I don't know anything about the hotline volunteer I spoke with in 2018, aside from their voice, which was beautiful and kind. I remain grateful for their time and care.

On to happier subjects… Vast amounts of joy went into this book, too. Above all, the joy of my life: My friends.

Thank you to those who read drafts of this book over the last years — Lisa Vogel, Anna Fechtig, Paulina "Daddy" Cassimus, Lou Griffith-Jones, and Nikki Butcher. Your feedback (and long chats when I needed to stop staring at poems) was invaluable. *Herzlichen Dank* to Lisa for your German edits, and to Luke Swenson for so adeptly translating "Welcome to Berlin!"

Paige Smith and Ceri Savage are two immense editors and writers I am lucky to call friends. Paige guided me at the start of this book (before I knew what it might become) and Ceri helped me to tie up all of the loose ends.

Thank you to the poets and editors who shaped these pieces, and who have been generous in their encouragement: Angela Carr, Erin Fornoff, Ana Paz, Zero Pilnik, Kevin Higgins, Gianluca Avanzato, and Cat Hepburn.

Thank you to Fern Angel Beattie for believing in this collection. I knew from the moment I first heard you speak about Write Bloody UK that I wanted to work together! It has been a supreme gift, and I can't wait to see what this next year holds for all of the WBUK poets.

Thank you to my original teachers. The glorious Patricia D'Alessandro taught me as much about life and love as about poetry. I wish I could share these poems with her now and listen to her play tunes on her upright piano while I sit on her couch and dream.

Kip Fulbeck taught me to be braver, and that it will always be a better gig if you can bond with the sound guy over classic rock music.

My mother, Rosi, knew I would be a writer before I did. My dad, Michael, started teaching me to write passionate, righteous letters in my girlhood. Thank you both for being enthusiastic about my creative pursuits, even when I gave you reasons to worry. I know you are always on my team.

Six wild women — my six howling wolves — also guided me, pushed me, inspired me to run after my dreams in the midst of global uncertainty. This book is for you all: Katherine, Kate, Polly, Rhian, Beatriz, Linda. For your dazzling, collective flame, for bringing me safely through the woods.

To my beautiful colleagues at Rose Bruford, and to my "Lads," thank you for your love, support, and laughter in this past half-year. I could choose no better group of actors to roll around on the floor with. You make "a July's day short as December."

Thank you to Maria Cassar for bringing some of these poems to life with movement, and to Zoë Waites for your generosity and care as I balanced The Bard with The Book. It would not be what it is without your support.

A huge thank you is in order for the generous individuals who have uplifted my work through Patreon over the last two years. You are my very own "small machine."

I have encountered a number of incredible people while performing poetry and would like to express my gratitude to all of the poetry organisers who have welcomed me at home and abroad. In particular, thank you to Helen and Bonita at Glastonbury for taking a chance on me and giving me my first opportunity in the UK. Thank you to the Quinlans and to all of my Irish poetry family for giving me shelter during my year of wandering.

Last but not least, there are the Berliners. Thank you to Annika and Tim for being my first friends and my makeshift Berlin family. To Sabina, Dominique, Maria, Emilie, Vicente for being my sounding boards (and for listening to hours of meandering voice messages). To Saide for giving me a peaceful place to finish my manuscript and a soft landing into London. Thank you, Elizabeth. Thank you, Ty. Thank you, Gus. All of your love has kept me afloat.

And there is Berlin, the place I feel equal parts possessed by and possessive of. Would I do it all again? No, but I wouldn't trade a second of it, either.

I am honored to share a birthday with a radiant star who once sang:

Ich hab' noch einen Koffer in Berlin, der bleibt auch dort und das hat seinen Sinn…

London,
January 30, 2022

Write Bloody UK would like to give special thanks to angel donor Sohrab Mehta.

Publication Notes

My heartfelt thanks goes to the editors who first selected these poems for publication and broadcast:

"A Cure for the Common Cold" — *Porter House Review*

"City Girls" and "In the Telling of It" — *ROPES Literary Journal*

"did you hear about mom?" — *The Selkie*

"Ex at the Museum," "I Know How to Love," "Yell Out" (under the title "Ten Years Ago He Called Out My Name") and "Ode to Sommersprossen" — *The Punch Magazine*

"Eyelashes" — broadcast on *Salma El-Wardany and LionHeart*, BBC Radio London

"feel free" — *The Waxed Lemon*

"Mourning, Day 28" — *Pendemic*

"Not sure if there's a ghost" — *Banshee*

"On the weekend Biden wins the election" and "Son of a Fish" (under the title "I Am a Fish") — *Figure 1*

"Open House: Two Rooms" — *Women Writing Berlin Lab Magazine*

"Porridge" — published in *The Times* UK and broadcast on *Today*, BBC Radio 4, as a part of poet Liv Torc's Haiflu Project, a collection of haikus and images created during the COVID-19 pandemic

"Snowfall in a Pandemic" — *Pen to Print*

"Summer Ad Infinitum" — broadcast on the 2019 Belfast Poetry Jukebox

"Twenty-Six" — *Magma*

"Who Else but Her?" — *NonBinary Review*

About the Author

DEMI ANTER is an Austrian-American writer and performer. Her work has appeared in *Magma*, *Banshee*, *Ninth Letter*, *Figure 1*, and *The Times* UK as well as on BBC Radio London. She has been a featured performer at Glastonbury Festival, Electric Picnic, the Scottish Storytelling Centre, and Poetry Ireland. After five years in Berlin, she now lives in London where she is completing an MFA at Rose Bruford College of Theatre & Performance.

www.demianter.com